Piles of Salt:

A Life Narrative of Civil War, Refugeeism, and Sociopolitical Transnationalism

Patrice M. Niltasuwan

This manuscript is dedicated to
all who risked their lives to
enrich America's kaleidoscope
and to those who died trying.

May you all have found peace.

CONTENTS

AUTHOR'S NOTE

To ensure the privacy of all individuals mentioned in the following account, pseudonyms, sans the names of large cities such as Pakse (Paxse) and other well known places and people, have been used. All pseudonyms, including his own, were created by the narrator, "Casey". Although this is a true account of one man's life journey and experiences, any names and/or situations that are identical to another's is purely coincidental.

The memories of the main character have been retold to the best of the author's ability with the most minimal of alterations. In some cases dialogue has been edited per the author's discretion to facilitate comprehension and fluidity. However, care has been taken to preserve with all integrity the elements of the actual account, dialogue and otherwise, as recalled by the narrator.

INTRODUCTION

Examination of immigration in the United States is essential to understanding both American policy and culture, in the historical and contemporary contexts. The contemporary American immigrant population contains an ever-expanding array of diverse peoples with equally diverse histories. Motives for immigration to the United States range vastly, from employer-sponsored, to political refugee, and a host of alternative conditions in between. In the latter half of the twentieth century, U.S. policy began differentiating newcomers by labels of either immigrant or refugee.[1] A person who fled their homeland (by choice or by force) in search of asylum elsewhere due to threat of personal danger by persecution or war[2] became subcategorized as a refugee. The rapid political restructuring of ideologies, geographies, and peoples following WWII produced the idiom refugeeism; thus intrinsically making refugees a phenomenon created within the political sphere.[3] Consequently, this new politically-constructed

---

[1] David R. Howell. "Refugee Resettlement and Public Policy: A Role for Anthropology."*Anthropological Quarterly*, (1982): 119.
[2] Cheryl Benard. "Politics and the Refugee Experience." *Political Science Quarterly,* (1986): 617.
[3] Scott Edwards. "The Refugee in International Society." *Political Science Quarterly*, (2010): 758.

Introduction

demographic quickly became a figure of intense interest during the final decades of the twentieth century.[4] The age of globalization has continued to affect change in various paradigms beyond the political and private, such as the social and academic.

As demography of the United States continues to be a subject of increasing interest, immigration (and refugee) studies have mutually gained greater attention. Appropriately, research surrounding the topic has become conceptualized from a more contemporary approach with the aim of inclusiveness of varied viewpoints, objectives, and motives, to discern the impact it has on today's society and the prospective future of the country. As such, current psychological and sociological research is primarily directed at assisting immigrant and refugee populations during the physical resettlement and emotional adjustment periods. However, anthropological research has the most potential for a mutually beneficial relationship with the field of refugee studies.[5] Given that the most populous wave of refugees entered the U.S. following the Vietnam War, much of the contemporary research

---

[4] Aihwa Ong. *Buddha is Hiding* (Berkley: University of California Press, 2003), 78.
[5] B. E. Harrell-Bond & E. Voutira. "Anthropology and the Study of Refugees." *Anthropology Today*, vol. 8, no. 4 (1992): 6.

surrounding this group is being directed towards longitudinal studies.

The conventional concept of what depicts a 'space' is "dependent on images of break, rupture, and disjunction."[6] This description is also applicable to the issue of defining what constitutes a fieldsite in contemporary anthropology. Given the aforementioned analogy, it can be further argued that within a solitary personal narrative lies a multi-sited ethnography – a particularly accurate assessment when reconstructing the life histories of any particular demographic of immigrant/migrant if we are to place their lived-experience within the framework of international historical events.

From a contemporary world perspective inclusive of innumerable diasporas, transnational flow and exchange of culture and populations, it is clear that personal identities have become increasingly deterritorialized.[7] Therefore, the precarious and unforeseen situations a war refugee encounters as a result of political agency forces identity reconstruction and allegiance reformation. Moreover, "physical movement from one space to another, the act of displacement, the act of

---

[6] Akhil Gupta and James Ferguson. "Beyond "Culture": Space, Identity, and the Politics of Difference." *Cultural Anthropology,* 7:1 (1992): 6.
[7] M. Franquiz, quoted in LeCompte, "The Transformation," 294.

reconceptualizing the hybrid identity, continues in an active way and does not end;" rather, the diverse facets of previous and present fuse together, forming a new, equally malleable identity. [8]

The complexity of this transformative process for refugees lies within the struggle to exist between perceptions of self and other, and where one is psychologically situated in relation to the past, present and future.[9] In response to external forces, (e.g. altered environment, status, language, and culture), internal transformation is unavoidable. Flexibility and determination must be exercised in tandem to successfully navigate life within an alien country/culture. In the case of an international refugee with few other options, such characteristics are absolutely imperative to their survival.

A multitude of refugee studies, primarily within the field of psychology, have sought to examine and explain the resilience displayed by refugees in regards to mindset and adaptation both during, and following traumatic events. The number of Southeast Asians who took refuge in the U.S. as a result of the Vietnam War

---

[8] Katrina M. Powell. "Rhetorics of Displacement: Constructing Identities in Forced Relocations." *College English 74.4* (2012): 300.
[9] *Ibid.*, 7.

totaled 581,000 during the 1980s.[10] On the whole, this faction of immigrants not only incurred some of the most severe effects of warfare, but has also shown a particularly remarkable degree of resilience. Laos alone received the equivalent of "one bombing mission every eight minutes, twenty-four hours a day, for nine years"[11] from the United States military. Although the goal of such excessive force was aimed at preventing the successful spread of communism in the region, the Laotian civilians were those most heavily affected.[12]

Despite the severe situational trauma and stress caused by the destruction and loss associated with war, Southeast Asian refugees in the United States appear to have coped remarkably well. According to previously published longitudinal studies, they (as a group) display no melancholy, and are considered to have become both psychology and socially well-adjusted within their new environments.[13] Southeast Asian cultures primarily practice Theravada Buddhism; therefore focusing on the present, as opposed to the past, has become an inherent cultural convention.

---

[10] Roger Daniels. *Guarding the Golden Door: American Immigration Policy and Immigrants Since 1882.* (New York: Hill & Wang, 2004),215.
[11] Channapha Khamvongsa & Elaine Russell. "Legacies of War: Cluster Bombs in Laos." *Critical Asian Studies* 41:2 (2009): 282.
[12] *Ibid.*, 290.
[13] Peter Sudefeld. "Reactions to Societal Trauma: Distress and/or Eustress." *Political Psychology*, 18:4 (1997): 857.

Introduction

The generally successful adaption of this particular group of immigrants could also be attributed to "the heightened concern of East Asians with social harmony [which] has been used to explain their greater tendency to rely on personal adjustment and accommodation rather than direct influence over the environment in meeting the challenges of everyday life."[14] More specifically, the fortitude and flexibility exhibited by those survivors who were displaced during the Laotian civil war may be due to the cultural mindset of embracing migration, as it has been a longstanding practice in Lao culture to relocate while in search of improved living conditions or opportunity.[15]

The proceeding story utilizes ethnography to focus on U.S. immigration through a narrated life history of an individual Laotian refugee. The advantage of situating a biographical narrative at the nucleus of historical events is the personal dimension added to the existing statistical data available relating to both the particular and similar events experienced by the narrator.

---

[14] R. Tafarodi, C. Lo, S. Yamaguchi, W.S. Lee, and H. Katsura. "The Inner Self in Three Countries." *Journal of Cross-Cultural Psychology.* (2004), 99.

[15] Andrea Savanda. *Laos a Country Study.* (Washington, D.C.: U.S. Government Printing Office, 1995), 93.

vi

As an applicable anthropologic methodology, oral history didn't begin to realize its maturation (via support by anthropologists such as Clifford Geertz) until the 1970s. In the 21st century it has become a thriving, viable, methodology and has proven its usefulness and applicability to an extensive range of topics.[16] One of the key reasons that oral history is increasingly embraced as a methodology is its ability to represent diverse perspectives that were previously absent or ignored when chronicling world history. Oral history ethnography has proven to be a most efficacious catalyst for bringing the voices of the underprivileged, the marginalized, and the conquered into being.[17] However, due to its dependence on the recollection of the narrator, the methodology has still encountered some skepticism in regards to its ability to provide exact details of events.[18] Despite any of its shortcomings, oral history is nonetheless an indispensible tool to advance our knowledge of the human condition and the world around us.

---

[16] Thomas Lee Charlton, Lois E. Myers and Rebecca Sharpless, eds., *Thinking about Oral History* (USA: AltaMira Press, 2008), 26.

[17] Thompson, *The Voice*, 7.

[18] David Palmer. "Every Morning before You Open the Door You Have to Watch for that Brown Envelope: Complexities and Challenges of Undertaking Oral History with Ethiopian Forced Migrants in London, U.K." *The Oral History Review*, 37:1 (2010): 37.

Introduction

By personalizing world events through the voice of one who experienced them first-hand, a new perspective arises as the events themselves become understood at a more intimate level. Furthermore, a single account of an incident or moment in time can be used as a transmitter of human history that speaks in part for the voiceless others who experienced similar events, as well as providing the human nucleus necessary to more fully understand an otherwise complex event and/or issues.[19]

Although each life history is unique, the following narrative will certainly share commonalities with some of the life experiences of the other 360,000+ refugees that migrated from Laos between 1975 and 1992.[20] Also, by utilizing the life-history approach, we gain the capacity to develop a more compassionate understanding of those among us who have experienced refugeeism regardless of the particulars of causation or origin.

---

[19] Paul Thompson, *The Voice of the Past* (Oxford: Oxford University Press, 2000), 269-270.
[20] Savanda, *Laos*, 92.

PROLOGUE

How does an individual maintain a secure sense of self, community, and culture throughout such enormous life changes such as civil war and forced migration? As people and their life experiences are no longer stationary in geographical location, contemporary life histories often encompass an array of environments and cultures. Therefore, the precarious and unforeseen situations the refugee encounters as a result of war forces identity reconstruction and allegiance reformation as well as the usual somatic and affective stresses and obstacles associated with assimilation such as language and learning to navigate the new social and political systems.

To explore contemporary transnationalism within the context of refugeeism, I have compiled the life-history account of a Laotian war refugee/immigrant to the United States. His story has been recreated in the following pages after many months of recorded interviews and personal discussions. Although perhaps subtle, the essence of anthropological inquiry into the above mentioned issues of displacement and globalism provide the framework for which this project was undertaken.

Prologue

The orator of the proceeding memoir is now over 70 years old and has been living in the United States for more than three decades. He has been a close family friend for over ten years. Throughout the history of our relationship, he had occasionally discussed with me his experiences of war, internment, escape, and subsequent relocation in the United States. In Southeast Asian culture it goes against social propriety to speak of the misfortunes one has experienced, as well as to discuss the past at any great length or in detail; this is particularly true for males. As a result there is a shortage of personal narratives from this group in all areas of refugee studies. However, when approached with the proposition to have his life history recorded, Casey (his personally chosen pseudonym) showed enthusiasm and remained an energetic storyteller committed to production of the memoir since its commencement. I have found his story to be quite captivating and one worth retelling.

Casey grew up on a family farm that was only one hundred feet from the banks of the Mekong River in southern Laos. He considered his childhood idyllic. The house which his father and mother had built together many years before Casey's birth was a simple one. Typical rural communities in Laos relied heavily upon arable ground along existing waterways for irrigation and transportation; this ensured sustainability while maintaining traditional lifestyle devoid of modern infrastructure. As generations upon generations had experienced before his family, Casey grew up along the banks of the Ma Nom Kong. In Lao, the name translates as Mother River Kong. The river was the source of life for the villages that settled along it from the mountains of Tibet to the South China Sea. The Mekong was an integral part of the community and of every person who lived along it. Casey, reflecting on the Mekong, affectionately said, "No river, no life."

Prologue

Casey's life along the Mekong began in 1939, when Laos was still officially a part of French Indochina. Throughout the next three decades he would live to witness his homeland gaining autonomy from the French to become the independent monarchy renamed the Kingdom of Laos, and eventually the communist-ran country of the People's Democratic Republic of Laos (Lao PDR). He was born on the brink of sweeping changes in Southeast Asia; the colonial era was nearing its final days, only to be replaced by the global political turmoil of World War II and the ensuing Cold War era.

The southern Lao life along the Mekong that Casey recollects was of a simpler time. It was a time when families were united and self-sufficient farming was an ordinary way of life. Despite tumultuous politics, villagers along the southern Mekong had enjoyed a simple way of life as far back as anyone could remember, and any folktale could recount. Families considered less fortunate than Casey's lived further from the river and depended on public wells for water. However, that auspicious location along the bank of Mother River soon turned from a sight that heralded 'home', to one that represented both confinement *and* freedom.

The river that served as the natural and political boundary between Thailand and Laos became a beacon of hope and freedom for many Laotians during the Vietnamese, Laotian, and Cambodian civil wars. Crossing the Mekong became a constant dream of most Laotians, a waterway to a new life for some, and a death bed for many. When the Lao civil war broke out as communism stormed across the country from Vietnam, fleeing Laos for the safety of non-communist Thailand became not only a daily imagining, but a necessity for survival for many Laotians; for those who opposed the communist regime, crossing the Mekong was their only chance of survival. Crossing the river to reach the western shore (Thai territory) was not only physically arduous and emotionally difficult, but often a futile effort for many never reached the other side. The communist soldiers kept a vigilant watch over the river and any movement in the waters was met with gunfire.

For Casey, crossing the river meant probable death, but staying in Laos meant certain death. It was not an uncommon sight to see bodies floating down the river and past the once peaceful homesteads of years past during the civil war years. Casey spent much of his time in the forced labor camp dreaming of how and when he would cross that river and never look back.

Prologue

Eventually he would succeed in his crossing - not just once, but many times.

At one point during the course of interviewing, Casey had expressed his desire to record what had happened to him during the civil war years in Laos and give a copy to all of his extended family. I proposed that we do just that. Initially he shrugged his shoulders and looked up from his hands that were clasped in his lap and said, "No, I can't. It's not right to do." However, since completion of the book, he now eagerly awaits the tangible form of his story to share with his family and friends. The following pages hold the story of the missing years in Casey's life history that he has yet to share with his family. It is my sincerest wish that I have retold his story honorably, and with the respect with which it deserves.

All changes,

Even the most longed for,

Have their melancholy;

For what we leave behind us

Is a part of ourselves;

We must die to one life

Before we can enter another.

- ANATOLE FRANCE

1

Rice fields & Monasteries

I was born in 1939. I grew up in the rice field. My father and mother had a rice field – a rice paddy. They owned that property. We didn't have much money. We had no money to hire people to help in the fields, so we just farmed it ourselves. There were four of us kids. My only brother died. He died in 1960. He was thirty-five or thirty-six…something like that. Some people killed him with magic. They put things like nails in his body. He was killed with magic - like voodoo or whatever you call it here. He was killed with a bad spell. I don't know why they killed him. He was a good guy, a really good guy with no enemies or *nothing*, so I don't know why somebody did that. The monks who prepared his body after he died told me that they pulled out some leather and a couple of nails from inside his body. Yep, it was *real* magic. Somebody really used magic to kill him! I don't know what happened to him, but my father…he knew. He knew something about it, but not me, I never really knew what happened.

My brother was still a monk at that time. He was living in the monastery. He went away to the Buddhist temple at twelve years old to work and to study. At age twenty-two he became the abbot of the temple, and then went to Thailand to study more with the monks over there. He was gone about seven years. He came home in 1958 and died in 1960. He moved back to the monastery when he got back from Thailand and that is where he died. Someone killed him.

He was the oldest kid of my parents, then there was a daughter born, but I never knew her – she died before I was born. She was about four or five years old, I guess. I don't know how she died, and don't know nothing about her. She got sick with something. We didn't have medicine back then. We just used herbs. I was born two years after she died. I never heard what her name was. We didn't talk too much about the dead, and we still don't. There is no need.

My brother was about seven when I was born, then came two younger sisters. I was the oldest at home when we worked on the farm. My brother had already moved away to live and study at the monastery by the time I was old enough to remember. Just my mother, father, and me worked in the fields and did everything.

My younger sisters just played all the time. Until I was twelve years old, I worked at home in the fields with my mother and father, then at twelve I went to study with the monks too, so I also became a monk – but just for a little while.

I think I was twelve when I went to the monastery. My brother died there, but that was after I finished my studies and left. He was already the leader of the monastery when I moved there. I was the youngest one, and some guys were as old as twenty-five, but that was about it. I remember at night it was so cold there, and in the daytime very hot – lots of sun – very hot! In the day time we studied. Our studies began early in the morning. We were taught by the monks. We studied everything – reading, writing, math, and the Buddhist books. A friend of mine was a teacher there because he had studied there a lot longer than me – he was really good. Oh, he helped me a lot! He studied really hard and was a good monk. Some people were not so good.

I went to the same monastery that my brother had studied at, but by then he was gone to Thailand. He returned to run our monastery for the last two years I was there. I lived and studied with the monks for seven years. No other schools were around because our town was too far from a city. We only had the monastery to go to if we wanted to learn. My parents didn't have to pay for me to study there because all the people in the towns around there would donate everything for the monks: food, clothes, money… everything we needed.

There were about twenty of us studying at the monastery when I was there. We were all different ages, and it was a place for boys only, you know. Girls didn't have nowhere to go study. They just stayed home and learned to take care of the house and fields with the parents. Girls didn't learn how to read or write or nothing like that then. I liked living at the monastery. It was better than working in the rice fields, but I didn't want to stay a monk my whole life like my brother. I have a certificate from there, from 1960. saying I completed my studies. I am proud of that - proud that I went to school, because not everybody did.

The monastery was a one day walk away from my family's house. We got time off to go visit our families a couple times every school year. We could go for the little visits – like two or three weeks at a time. Usually I would go alone to visit my mom and dad and help in the fields. Sometimes my brother would go with me, but most of the time he had to stay there to run the temple. He was the big leader then. He was the abbot. His name was Venna.

We had to wear robes over our whole body. We wore the orange ones. Just like the monks you see in the pictures – we had to wear robes like that, and shave all our hair off. We didn't have time to play. We had to study all day, but we all lived together so we talked at night after we went to our sleeping area. We talked about what we had learned from monks every day. No one ever talked about anything fun, just our studies.

Every day at the monastery was the same. We all had jobs there – we all had jobs we had to take care of. Everybody had to work to take care of the monastery and temple. We were each told what areas we had to clean. I hated getting up in the morning at five o'clock to study. We had to study for an hour and then start cleaning things up around the monastery. The big leaders there didn't want to do nothing, so the students had to take care of everything.

At seven a.m. all of us young monks had to go walk around town carrying big bowls. We had to walk down every street in town together in one big group. We walked in the road and people came out of their houses to give us the donations. We never went up to the houses, or inside anyone's house, or asked for anything from anybody. We only walked past the houses and if people wanted to donate some food to us they would come out to put it in our bowls. If you didn't go, you would go hungry – nobody would give you their part of the food from that morning. We ate once in the morning and we ate again at noon. We would keep some of the food that people gave us in the morning and save it to eat for our lunch. That was the only time we got to eat when we lived there. After we got back from doing the morning walk around the town to collect food, we went back to the monastery to eat. After breakfast we all had to go start our study time.

People donated all kinds of food. They just put them all together in the big bowls: rice, meat, vegetables, whatever. We only ate in the morning and at noon – no eating at night. At night time we just had coffee, so we only ate two times a day, but that was better than some of the other temples. At some temples they only ate once a day – Oh, I couldn't stand that! Eating just two times a day I almost died, you know? But it was ok because we could drink lots of water, and coffee, too. We didn't have things like apple juice, or orange juice, no nothing like that – just coffee or water – that's all we had. I liked to put the cream and sugar in my coffee if we had it, but sometimes people didn't give us no sugar or milk, and we were just the monks with no money, so we had to drink it black.

When people gave us money we saved it to buy the milk for our coffee. We had to save a lot to buy that milk. We couldn't use much at one time either – only one or two spoons for our coffee. Sometimes, if people had a big party at their house, and a lot of it left over, they would donate some milk to us…but that didn't happen much. The only milk in Laos was in a small can. It was from France.

Before our people didn't have nothing. The whole country was so poor. Now they have milk in a bottle, and everything. Oh my god, I am never hungry now when I go there like I was before! There is all kind of food imported from Vietnam, and China, and Thailand too – so much food – Oh my god! When I was young, people had cows, lots of cows, but we didn't know how to milk them then. My cousin had thirty cows, but didn't know how to get the milk from them. Nobody drank cow's milk. We thought it was just for the baby cows. We didn't know anything, but now they know everything!

Now Lao people have cow's milk, goat's milk, and all kinds of things. My people eat everything now too: goat, sheep, dog, and cat. But, if you believe in the monk and in the Buddha, you can't eat the cat, monkey, dog, tiger, lion, or snake. Monks can't eat those animals. They never did. Those animals were made by a god to take care of the Buddha. You can eat chickens or cows…its ok. Right now the other people eat every-thing though – dogs, snakes, all of that, but the monks still don't. Now my country has restaurants that sell the

7

dog meat only: dog meat, barbeque dog, all that. People ask me if I want to go and I say, "No way!" I never ate that before and I don't want too. I never ate the dog or snake. No. Never! Dog was always popular to eat, but my father told me, "Don't eat that." So I never touched it. I ate eel before, but never the snake. My dad said, "If you believe in the Buddha you don't eat that kind of stuff." He told me it said in the Buddha's papers, "If you want to see the god don't eat that stuff." So I never touched it. Just the eel. It's a little bit like a snake, but it's not a real snake, so it's ok for me. It's good.

I wasn't really happy being a monk, but it was ok, because I wanted to study. Once a year we could go home to stay at our family's house for three months: July, August, and September. We got that time off to go home. During the school year we always had to be back to the temple by night time. If you needed to go anywhere it was ok during the day, but at night time you had to be back inside. It was only at the break time that we could go to stay with other people, or stay at other temples to study with other monks.

Every year they would give us a big test before we went home for the break. When we were on our break we didn't have to do any studies. The big monks from the temple, they sent us the note to our house to tell us it's time to come back to school. Sometimes when I went home to visit my parents they would give me money to take back if they had it, but usually they didn't have any. It took me one whole day to walk home. If I left at six a.m., I could be there by six p.m., but sometimes I got lazy and found a temple to sleep at, then I had to finish walking home in the morning.

Sometimes I rode the boat home, but it cost money, and us monks didn't really have any. Today you can make that same trip in one or two hours by car or bus. There aren't too many taxi boats no more. Before there were lots of boats... *so* many boats on the Mekong! Oh, so many! Sometimes the men who drove the boats would let the monks ride for free. They didn't want to take money from the monks – it's better to get the good luck from the Buddha for helping the monks.

At the monastery it was all men. There were no ladies around, just *talk* of ladies. When I went home for the break I would talk to ladies sometimes, but just do some talking, not looking for a girlfriend, you know? I was a monk, so no way – I couldn't do that! Sometimes I visited my friend's house and the ladies there would make us food. I liked talking to them when they were cooking. Oh, I liked that a lot. Oh, nice ladies! They would cook us fish... chicken ...whatever they cooked, I liked it a lot!

When all the monks were together we couldn't talk about the ladies, only talk about studying. If they caught you talking about the ladies? Oh, you got in big trouble! We could only *think* about ladies. Hahaha! We just did thinking, thinking, thinking. The only ladies around there were in our minds. I thought about the ladies a lot. Oh, I liked to do that! Some of the monks would talk with me about ladies, but I was scared, too. I didn't want to get in any trouble, either.

We couldn't have girlfriends, and we couldn't get drunk there either, nope. No ladies and no drink. We just had water, so after seven years I didn't want to stay there anymore. I really wanted a family and monks can't have families. I wanted to finish my studies and leave there to find a job. I wanted a family – I *needed* a family. My pole stood up all the time. You know what I mean? I was a young man then.

2

The Policeman in Pakse

After I left the monastery in 1960, I went back to live with my parents and my sisters. I was looking for a job after I went home. I needed money. I had to walk to other towns to look for work because we didn't have a car then. No one had cars then, and no bus came to our village, like now. To walk to the big cities it took one or two days to get there. We didn't even have a bicycle in my family. They were expensive and my family had no money. But, we did have a telephone, and one day someone called the house and asked if anyone living there wanted to become a policeman. That was about two or three months after I came home from the monastery. I needed a job, so I just said yes. My sisters stayed to help my parents with the rice field, then one got married and moved out. The youngest, Mong, she never got married. She lived with my parents forever. I don't know *why* she never got married. Right now she stays

11

by herself in my mom and dad's old house – not the same one we grew up in, but the house they were living in when they died.

Yep, it was 1960 when I went to study at the policeman school. Before I could become a cop I had to go to another city to do the special police training school. The policeman training took two years, and it was really hard. The training was in the closest big city, Pakse. I had a cousin that lived there, so I stayed with him when I studied at the police school. His name was Hang. He was also a policeman. He had been a cop for a long time, and was a big boss by the time I got there. For on-the-job training we had to train with a partner who had been a cop in the big city for a long time. Oh, it was such hard work! That's how I came to Pakse. That's where the police were then.

In Pakse they had buses, and I rode in my first taxi there too. They had cars and everything there – but only some people in the big cities had cars then, not like my small town where nobody had a car before. Some people in Pakse had a lot of money, and they had cars to drive out to visit the smaller towns. They didn't have to ride the bus or walk like the rest of us. My cousin was like that. He had two or three cars. Oh, Hang was very rich! I never had my own car, but loved to ride with him. I didn't care where, as long as we were in the car. I never had a car in Laos. No one like me ever had a car. I didn't really drive a car too much until I got to America. My cousin let me drive his car a little bit, but not much. He was afraid I would fuck up his car – and so was I, because he would have killed me! Now they have lots of cars in Laos.

I finished the police training in 1962. I lived with my cousin and his wife there for a long time in Pakse. I lived with them until I got married and had to move out and rent a house. My new wife and I moved in together after we had a wedding. I still didn't have much money then, so I had to talk with my cousin and borrow some money so I could pay the rent for our first apartment there. Her name was Dang, and she was friends with my cousin's wife. After the first time I met her I asked my cousin's wife, "Can I marry her?" She didn't answer me. All she said was, "You are a bad boy." It was true, really I was kind of a bad boy then. She was 19 and I was 24. She was from the other side of the city, but her hometown was a small town too, just like me. She was in Pakse visiting, but she lived at home still in the smaller city with her mom and brothers. She helped them work their rice fields.

In 1963 I got married to Dang. Even after we got married she would still go home for two or three months at a time to help her family. While she was gone I was a bad boy. I was always going somewhere, you know what I mean? I was always doing "something". I still liked the ladies a lot. Oh, I probably liked them too much.

My wife's dad, he was already passed away when we got married. He had stomach cancer, I think. He died at 55. There was no one else to help the mom then. There were still four or five brothers that lived at home with her, but my wife was older than them so she had to go help her mom too. I sent money with her when she went home to help her mom and brothers. She had seven brothers, but some were older and had got married already and moved out. After they got married they didn't come back to help no more because they had to help their wife's family instead – that was the same with me, too.

I quit going home to help my parents and had to start taking care of my wife's mother and brothers. Sometimes I went to help, but I was working all the time in Pakse so I just sent the money for them instead of going to work in the fields. The son-in-laws were supposed to help in the rice fields too. From the money they paid me every month, I took some out to take to them. I gave my mom-in-law the money to send the younger boys to school. The schools were free, but you had to pay for uniforms, and food, and books. They went to a place like a boarding school where they had to live at to study because my wife's hometown had no schools.

During the war my wife's younger brothers went to learn from the communists in Pakse and became the party members. After they studied with the communists I don't know what they did, because I wasn't around no more. I was gone to the camp by then. I know her two youngest brothers now work in construction. I helped them all to go to school, and now they are doing really good! A lot of people, especially the young people, are doing really good and making a lot of money in Laos now…and they can all go to school now, too.

In 1975 they took over. That's when Laos became Communist. I don't know what day – I forgot about it, but it was in 1975. In 1968 the American army started asking for volunteers from the Lao police department to go fight the communists from North Vietnam. They offered to pay us double what the Lao government was paying us to be the policemen. I didn't want to join with them then. I didn't want to be the full-time soldier, but sometimes I would go. I would volunteer to go with them, but only for the short fighting missions.

The Policeman in Pakse

For the short mission assignment we would go with the American soldiers into the jungle and fight the communists there for three or four months. I joined with them sometimes to fight in the jungle, but I only did it for the money. They would pay us good, and we could go back to being just the policeman again when the mission was done. It was good money to take back and give to my family. Nobody had money then and we needed it. The Americans paid good! Some Thai people joined them too to fight the Commies because the money was really good money. The Lao government couldn't pay much because they were too poor – just like all the people. A lot of Lao policemen and soldiers that joined the Americans to fight got killed in the jungle. But, every time we finished the fighting mission and returned to the city, the Americans still paid the money they owed to the Lao soldiers – they paid their money to the families of all the men that died with them in the jungle. That was a good thing, you know? It was better than dying for nothing, right?

They wanted everyone to work together. They wanted us to join together with the army and fight the communists, so in 1970 the Lao government made all of us policemen become soldiers. They put me in the army in 1970. In '75 the communists put me in the jail. That's when I went to the prison camp.

3

The Plantation Prison

They captured me and took me to the prison camp in 1975. All the people who were working for the old government had to go to study Communism. All of us that had any kind of the government job, like us policemen, they took us all to the jail camp. We were supposed to learn the Commie culture...or something like that. In the camp we were taught about the North and South and why the communists *had* to take over, but the only thing in my head everyday was, "I have to go to Thailand." That's all I was ever thinking about. I just kept thinking, "How am I going to get out of here? How I am going to stay alive to get to Thailand?"

Some of the people in the camp with me I worked in the police department with, but people were brought to that camp from other cities too, so most of the people I didn't know when I got there. There were about six or seven hundred people there – many were police officers. The chiefs and captains had to go to a different camp – they couldn't stay with us. Like my cousin, Hang, he had to go to a different camp because he was a captain. He died in the prison camp. The king of Laos and all the big leaders were sent to a camp, too, and they all died together. People said all the leaders of the big cities went to a meeting in a house and the communists bombed the house. That's what I heard…they died in there.

The Commies didn't want to give me my freedom because I wouldn't learn how to be "with" them. I never learned the right Commie way, but I think they made it like that on purpose, you know? They gave us the test every month and asked us questions and said if we learned right we could leave, but it was a lie. I never had the right answers for them.

They were afraid we would get out and go fight with the rebel soldiers. Some guys played the game real good and they got to get out to go back home and work for the communists. Some people studied good – they studied really good, and got loose from there, but not me. Nope, they never told me I had the good answers.

We had to go study every day at a big meeting. We had to learn the Communist style…we studied the Communist rules every day. We had to listen to them every day and study what they said. Everyday – but I still didn't know the answers they wanted from me. Some of my answers were good, some bad. Sometimes I gave them a good answer, but nope, my answers were never good enough to get freedom. They told me all the time, "Nope, maybe next year." I tried to learn, but there were too many things to remember. We didn't learn one thing at a time - maybe like one hundred new rules a day! The communists had already been learning for 30 years when they took over my country, but it was all the new stuff to us, so how did we know? We were just regular guys. We didn't know nothing about the Commie rules. How could we learn it all in one day? I think they made it too hard because they didn't want to let people go – they needed us to tend the coffee fields and pick up bombs. Who was going to do that if we were free?

People could get free if they studied really good – but not me. I didn't want to study, you know? They asked the questions and wanted the answers, but I never had the *right* answers. Hahaha! They said, "Oh, what are you waiting for? Do you think your old boss will come save you? You want to join back with them, huh?" I said, "No, I don't want to join with anybody. I just want to go home and stay with my family." Every time they always told me the same thing: Later, later, later! Two times a month we had to go to be questioned, and two times a month I had the wrong answers. I couldn't get out of there.

My wife came to visit me in there – in the camp – three or four times, but not the kids. She would bring me food and clothes. Our house was a long way away. She had to walk a long way to get to another city and then take a bus, and then walk again many miles to the camp. They wouldn't let any traffic get close to the camp. They would let her stay two or three nights with me. When my wife came to visit me in the camp I would tell her, "I want to go to Thailand," and she would say that it was up to me. She knew I had to go.

I saw her maybe once a year. I never saw my daughters or sons then. My mother-in-law watched the kids when she came to visit. My kids were all little when they put me in the camp. My youngest son, Thot, was born in 1972. Then my wife didn't have babies anymore. I think she didn't have any more eggs or something. My youngest baby was only one year old when I had to go away to the camp. My second daughter from Laos, Chan, lives here in America now. My kids were little when I had to go to the camp. I never saw my daughters or my sons for a couple of years. I never got to see them when I was in the camp.

They sent people home once a year to visit the family, or if the family was sick or something. You could go back home for visiting, but only for one week, then you had to go back to the camp. After I stayed in the camp for about two years I got to go home couple times to visit my family too. Everybody always came back when they went to visit the family because they made you sign a paper – a guarantee. They made the family sign it too. It was a guarantee that you will come back. People came back because they didn't want the family to get in trouble. If you didn't go back they would put the family in jail. I didn't want to stay with my family much because the dog barked every night, and I heard the gun shots. They were killing people every night. They said they were shooting the people who had escaped to Thailand and came back with guns.

In Thailand the rebels could get the guns there. At night time you have to stay in the house. It's not safe. If you go outside at night you have to have two or three people go with you. It's better not to go. Oh, it was hard there, you know? It was hard to go back and visit. Every time I went to visit I was thinking about not going back, but I did. I followed the rules. All night the dog would bark. At night the communists would come and look at the houses to see what people were doing.

The Plantation Prison

They were looking for me because they wanted control – they didn't want me to escape to Thailand, you know? They were always watching me – day or night, you never knew who was watching you. They came every night to check my papers, and sometimes every day. We had to carry the paper from the camp so they knew that we didn't escape. They had to see that we were just visiting and gonna go back to the camp. They would ask a lot of questions. They kept checking on me because they didn't want me to escape. They thought maybe I would escape to Thailand. I had to sign a new paper with them every day. Every day they would bring a new paper for me to sign that said I wouldn't escape to Thailand…sign one day, two days, three days – every day for a whole week promise the same thing.

I knew I couldn't ever go back to my family. My wife knew it too. If I was gonna escape I had to try to get to Thailand. I had no choice. If I escaped from the camp and got caught they would have killed me. When people tried to escape and got caught they would bring them back to the camp for the example and show everybody – they would make us all look at each of them in the eyes, then they would kill them that night.

One time I saw some of the people who got killed all in a big hole at the camp – about seventy people they all killed at one time! They were people that they caught who had tried to escape from the camp. They had been escaped for about two or three months, but they found them and showed us those guys when they brought them back to the camp. When they brought them around, they said, "See? Even if you escape, you're not done yet. We will still find you and kill you!" At night we would hear the gunshots...*bang, bang, bang, bang*!

One day when I was sent to get wood for cooking the rice I saw flies all over in the tall weeds and thought, "What the heck?" so I went to look where all the flies were to see what was going on and saw a big hole with seven people laying in it. They were all dead. They were the ones that had gotten killed three days ago. They were just left there – left to rot in the hole. It stunk so bad, and I thought, "Oh, my god." I just stared at them for a few minutes counting them and looking at their faces...*one, two, three, four, five, six, seven.* They weren't people from my camp. I didn't know those guys. They were people from some other camp. I think escaped from a northern camp and got caught down south near my camp. They had been brought to my camp to be killed. Even if you escaped a camp, you weren't done yet.

When the Commies caught rebels or the people that escaped from some other camps they would bring them to our camp and call a meeting for all of us to go to. They would have a big meeting in the field when they would bring people in to kill. The Commies would show them to us and say, "You want to die, then try to go. You will never escape us!" So who wanted to go, you know? We were all scared. The guys they caught were scared and looked upset. They were getting ready to die, so they looked *really* upset.

Those men were all older than I was then. They marched them away after they walked them around and showed everybody. We all had to sit down on the ground and they walked them in front of each of us. They made them stand in front of each of us and warn us not to escape. They walked them all around the big field to speak to all 600 of us! The captured men said: "Don't try to escape, they will catch you and you will be killed like me," and then they said, "Sorry." to everybody. They had to tell to everybody, "If you escape you will die! I will die soon too because they caught me." We just sat on the ground and listened to them and said, "Ok, ok." It was really terrible, but all those meetings still didn't stop people from trying to escape. People didn't listen to them.

Every time they would catch new ones they would call a big meeting again and bring the new prisoners around to show us. After that they would then put them all in a big army truck and show them around to everyone in the town. I don't know what they did with the ones they took away like that. I only ever saw one of the captured prisoners again – it was in the refugee camp in Thailand. I asked him what happened to him when they took him away. He said they took him to another camp for about six months and then he got away because he had some money brought to him from his family. He paid off the guards at the camp to let him sneak out....you know, they didn't watch him when he escaped. He went with a rebel soldier and escaped to Thailand. That was the only guy from the camp that I ever saw again. Only *one* guy. That's all. All those people in there, but I never saw any of them again.

If you were a soldier and got caught by the Commies you had to stay in the camp – with no money or nothing. They gave us food, but not much. They only gave us a little bit of food: about one cup of rice with salt on it, and maybe a banana from the jungle. It was only a little salt, just a little, little bit – it was the only flavor for rice we ever got. We could grow our own food if we wanted...if you got some seeds from home or somewhere. Every morning we had to get up really early if we wanted to work on the garden. There were no gardens when we got there. If we wanted to grow food we had to cut down some jungle and make a garden ourselves.

In the mornings we got to eat a little bit for breakfast (all we *ever* got to eat was breakfast). After breakfast we had to go to work in the coffee fields there. Sometimes we would cut bananas down from the trees, or cut down the banana trees and scoop out the inside and eat it. There were a lot of banana trees there, too. There was jungle all around the coffee fields. The prison camp area was really big - like a small city. One day I had to work in one area, maybe the next day they would send me to the other side of the camp a few miles away to do work.

Before we could make the coffee fields for them, first we had to cut the trees down in the jungle and put in all new plants. They had a few coffee plants there when we got there, but not too many. We had to make big coffee fields for the government. They still grow coffee there. It's a really famous kind of coffee bean in Asia now. They say it makes the coffee with the really sweet taste. They take people to do the tours of that place, but they don't tell the truth about it. I never went back to that place again when I went back to visit Laos after the war. I don't want to see it, no more, you know?

I took care of the coffee fields and took care of the bombs there in the camp, too. We had to pick them up and burn all the bombs that the Americans had dropped – about 4,000 bombs a day! We had to collect them all in a pile and make a fire to get rid of them. We worked taking care of the coffee plants and collecting the bombs when we found them – farming and picking up bombs at the same time. Every day we had to pick up the new bombs from the coffee fields. There was a whole bunch of bombs there. People got killed all the time from the bombs that fell in the coffee fields. Lots of people got killed from that. They were everywhere. We had to carry all the bombs to make big piles, then load them up to take them to Pak Song to burn. We couldn't burn them inside the camp.

If we found any bombs that didn't explode (usually the shell bombs) we took them to one of the big leaders in the camp. They collected them in a big house at the camp that we had to build for the bombs, and then sold them to Thailand. The communists didn't like Thailand, but nobody else wanted to buy them, you know? Cambodia had the same thing: war. Vietnam, same thing: war. All three countries had *too* many old bombs and war stuff, so we had to sell it to Thailand. I heard that Thailand bought all of it in 1985 after the war, but I don't know. I don't really know what happened to all of that stuff.

When it was time to burn them we had to put wood and all the bombs in a pile, then we yelled to everyone to get back, and we would start the fire. We put up a sign so nobody could go close to that area where we burned the bombs. They didn't want anybody to see the fire – that's why we burned them in Pak Song – a small town about 30 miles away. At noon every day we started the big fire. About 100 people worked in that area with me burning the bombs. The fires burned all day and all night until the next morning. We would start the fires at noon again with all the new bombs found that morning. Every day there were new bombs, and every day we made new fires. The bombs just kept coming. They came from airplanes and big guns for two or three years…never stopping.

In 1974 there was a lot of fighting in Pak Song. The U.S. army dropped a lot of bombs all day, all night, over there. Sometimes for weeks I didn't know if it was daytime or night time because I never saw the sky. The sky was just all black with smoke from too much fighting. There were so many times I didn't see the sky for a long, long, time...maybe for many months. Bombs and bullets were everywhere. Smoke was so thick in the sky, and there were bombs all over the ground, and the sound of the fighting never stopped.

It never stopped.

4

Across the Mekong

I escaped from the camp in '78. I got real sick in the camp. I never ate much for three years and it made me sick. Many people got sick and died there. I didn't eat anything – my stomach, oh it hurt so much after three years, you know? I was real sick. My legs couldn't stand up no more. I was sick for about three months and had to stay at the hospital inside the camp. I didn't get too much better so they sent me to the big hospital in town. They trusted me to go to the hospital and come back because I listened to them before and went back when they let me go visit my family. I stayed there in the big hospital for three days, and oh, I ate a lot! I felt a lot better, you know, because they gave me food there. But, after only three nights they wanted to send me back to the camp. They told me I could stay one more day then would have to go back to work at the camp the next day. When I found out where I was going I sent a message to a friend and he came to see me. He lived in the big city where the hospital was. I told him, "I want to go Thailand. Can you help me? I need your help. I don't want to go back to the camp." He said, "Ok." He had never been put in the jail. The communists didn't know about him, so he got to keep his freedom.

When I left the hospital they gave me a travel paper and told me to just go back to the camp. I just said, "Ok, I'm going, but I don't have no money for the bus, I need some money first." They gave me money – they gave me 10,000 kip (about $1.00), and I said, "Ok, I will go back to the camp now." I felt good. Why would I go back to the camp, you know? Hahaha! I saw the Mekong River and Thailand on the other side, how could I go back to the camp? I thought, "It's the time to go right now!" I talked to myself and said, "You have time right now, you will never have the time again." So when I left the hospital I just walked down the street but didn't go to the bus. I went to meet the friend of mine who was going to help me – he was going to take me to Thailand. We escaped together.

After I left the hospital and found my friend I stayed with him hiding at his house and other safe places with some other people for fifteen days waiting to go. We were all there waiting to escape Laos. We had to wait for the soldiers to come back to help us get out. We couldn't stay in any place more than one or two days because it wasn't safe. We had to keep moving and stay with different people. We had to keep moving, waiting for the rebel army to help us get through the jungle and across the river. We had to wait for the rebel army to come back across from Thailand so we can go back with them. There was a lot of fighting going on then. There was fighting every day and every night. All day and all night you heard the guns: big ones, small ones, everywhere the sound of guns. That's why we had to go hide and sometimes wait in the jungle, too. It was dangerous because anyone caught trying to escape was killed. If they had caught me, even hiding in the city when I was supposed to be back to the camp, they would have killed me. It was a scary time but I knew if I went back to the camp that I would die in there. I only had the one chance to live, and so I had to cross the river to Thailand.

During those fifteen days that I had to wait until my friend had everything ready for us to go, I snuck back to my old house to see my wife and kids two times. I knew I couldn't take the kids with me because it was too dangerous. If I took those kids we probably all would be dead now. We would have got killed. I didn't want to leave them. I wanted us all to stay together, but it was a dangerous war and so many people were being killed. Many families, they all died because the communists thought they might be against them or helping other people escape.

I didn't want to leave my family, but if I had stayed I would have been killed and they would have too. I was putting them in danger just because I went near them. I was very careful to not be seen by the soldiers when I went to talk to my wife. I told her I had to escape to Thailand, but I didn't talk to anybody else. She wanted to come with me and bring our kids but I said, "No! They will be killed! We will probably all die!" Her mother wanted her to go with me. My mother-in-law, she understood, she knew I would be killed if I stayed in Laos. She said that we should leave the kids with her and she would keep them safe and my wife and I should escape together, but my wife, she said no. There was no way would she leave the kids alone with her mom. I told her, "I'm not staying here no more. I have to go to Thailand." I asked her if she wanted to go with me, but she said, "No, I got three kids, and my mom is getting old. I can't go." Her mom wanted her to go, but my wife? Oh, she couldn't leave my kids, and she said her mom was getting old and who else was gonna help her? It was just too dangerous to take the kids, or her mom.

We knew that probably we would never see each other again. The chance that I would die was pretty good. Most people didn't make it to Thailand, but we knew I couldn't stay. If I had stayed I would have been killed. I would be dead now. When I got to Thailand I sent the letter back home to my wife with somebody that was going over there, but I didn't know for a long time if they got my letter or not.

Our friend who helped us escape had guns and everything hidden in the jungle. He knew his way through the jungle – he went back and forth, back and forth so many times. He helped a lot of people escape. He hid guns all through the jungle and when we would get to those places where guns and food were hidden we would stay there for the day and sleep. In the jungle we ate. He knew people who would come from the countryside towns - from the rice fields, and they would bring food to him. He would plan everything ahead and the people would help him and bring food. Of course not much food, but any little bit was better than none. That was the first time I escaped.

After I escaped the first time I became a rebel soldier, but not for too long, really. I went back to fight many times, but I went with a different group. The rebel soldiers had small army camps on the Thailand side of the Mekong. They would come back and forth fighting in Laos and then back to the safe camp in Thailand. It took three nights to get to Thailand from Pakse. We could only travel at night – during the daytime we hid in the jungle and slept. We had to hide. Oh, we met many bad guys in the jungle! We had to shoot them to get away. I had to kill many people. Oh, a lot of people. I had to, or they would have killed me.

If I didn't kill them they would kill me, you know?

My friend that escaped with me the first time, he stayed six months in the refugee camp in Thailand. Still, he kept saying he wanted to go back to see if his family was ok and he wanted to join with the fighting back there too. He went back to Laos with a couple other people and they caught him and killed him. He had a wife and kids. I don't know why he went back there! He was worried about his family so he just went back. He just always worry, worry, worry, that guy. We were different, you know? I went back to fight against the Communists too, but I never went to visit my family. No, no, I *never* tried to see them! I forgot about them. I had to forget all about it, you know?

I went back to Laos to fight with about eighty people the first time. I didn't want to go back with just three or four people and get killed like my friend did. I joined with another friend of mine who had been in the army for a long time. He used to be a communist too, but he escaped their army, and then joined a rebel army to go back to fight against them. Hahaha! He was different, you know?

In the refugee camp nobody had the guns, but we could get them outside the camp in Thailand. Sneaking to Laos was not good, you know, because they had the army all over. No, it was not good. We had to cross the river and then go through the jungle to fight. Every time we went back for fighting I thought to myself, "Oh, I'm gonna get back to the camp and not go back to do any fighting no more." We thought that someday the rebels would win and the communists would go away, but nope, it never happened. The people in Laos helped us with fighting in the jungle. They helped because they brought us food and everything. But sometimes, those people, they got killed for helping other people escape.

We only fought in the jungle for three or four nights at a time, then after that we went back to Thailand to a small army camp we set up. It was about eighty people in our small army with our own camp, but there were lots of groups and all fighting the communists, but the communists had camps too. We always went at night. In the jungle we heard fighting with guns all day and night. We had to hide during the day. After a few days in the jungle we all had to go back to the camp because we would run out of food. I didn't go fight every time they did. Sometimes I just stayed back at the rebel camp on the Thailand side of the river and didn't go fighting with them the next time they went.

There were twelve people in the group one time when we tried to cross. I went with the rebel group to help some other people escape from Laos. We were all going to escape from Laos together – across the Mekong River. We couldn't go no further after we got to the jungle because the fighting got too heavy. We waited two days in the jungle, but on the second morning the Commie soldiers started shooting. We all went together down to the river and blew our air in to the black plastic garbage bags we brought with us to help us float across the river. The people that were going to try to escape always hid the big black bag in their underwear because if you got caught with one they knew you were gonna escape and they would kill you. We held our black bags to our chests and walked out into the river to float across. The Commie soldiers started shooting into the river at us. I found a little island half way across the river and thought it would be a good place to stop and hide until night again because nobody could see me. Everybody in the group was separating. We didn't know if we were gonna die. You never knew. Sometimes we would meet up again on the Thailand side of the river – but everybody would scatter when they started shooting and we never knew where people went or who died. I think only one person in the group got killed that time.

After that trip, the one where I spent the day hiding on the island, I didn't want to go back to Laos no more. I had a lot of time alone that night and the whole next day hiding in the water. I just tried not to move or sleep and kept thinking, thinking, thinking. I had seen too many of the dead people floating down the river. I knew one day I would be them if I kept crossing the river too many times. I was asked if I wanted to go back and help some more with the rebel fighting, but I didn't want to do it no more. I wanted to get away from the war. I wanted to have a life again, and if I wanted to do that I knew I had to leave Laos for good and stop going back. I *had* to stop or I was gonna get killed.

I got sick. In the jungle we had to walk all day and all night – we couldn't sleep you know? We got back to the camp and I told them I wanted to go to the hospital because I was sick. I said I was sick, but I was really just sick in the head. Hahaha! I would just shake my head, "No, I'm not going back with you guys. I'm sick. I wanted to go to the hospital and they said, "Ok, you go and then come back here and help us keep fighting," but I never went back. Hahaha! I went to the refugee camp in Ubon – they had the hospital in there. I stayed there until I got better, but I didn't want to go back fighting no more.

I was sick of the jungle: walking all night, all day, never sleeping. Every day and night we had to keep hiding and fighting in the jungle, and mosquitoes all day and all night there too, you know? A lot of people got sick from the mosquitoes, and some people died from it. We just had to leave them in the jungle when they died. They were dead, you know? We couldn't do nothing. We couldn't burn them because we were hiding, so we couldn't make no fires or smoke or they would find us in there. So, most of the time we had to leave them there in the jungle, but sometimes we had the time to bury them.

Some people got their feet and legs hurt too – they had the bombs in the jungle. People would step on them and their legs would come off, so we had to carry them back to the camp in Thailand and help them. When people got hurt we went back in the whole group. We had to stay in the group. If we went back just three or four people at a time we would be killed. Some people died, you know? Some people died right away, so we left them in the jungle, but some people just got the leg cut off half way from the bombs, so that was ok – that was better – we could carry them back to Thailand. Then they had to be carried all the way back to the refugee camp to go to the hospital. In Ubon they had a hospital for helping people who got hurt like that. At the rebel soldier camp we only had the army doctor and he didn't carry much – we didn't have much medicine to help people when they got hurt too bad or when they got real sick.

My new wife – the one I met in the camp in Thailand – she said she crossed the river too to get there. Her whole family went together. There was about four or five families that all went together, and there was about four or five people in each family – it was like a party, you know? Hahaha! They lived near the border, so they all walked about two days – not too far from her house. They all walked all night, you know, about twenty people. They took cows and buffalo with them. They took all that with them. They took the cows and the water buffalo because they didn't had no money. In Thailand they could sell them for some money. That's all they had – no money – so they had to take the animals to get money later. In Thailand people would buy them, then they would have money to take to the refugee camp with them, you know? Everybody in her group, they all made it to Thailand ok. They knew where the army was, so they didn't go that way, and all of the families and the animals escaped ok.

The Mekong River was really "hot". People got killed all the time. You had to find out where the communist army was working every day – you had to find out! There was no communist army where they crossed the river at. They told me they didn't hear nothing – they crossed further north than me. When she first got to Thailand they all stayed in the Lao people rebel army camp too near the border. The Lao army had little camps set up all along the border in Thailand to help the people who escaped when they got across. They helped protect them. Thailand didn't want all the Lao people in their country. They needed to have the control in their country. They wanted all the Lao people to stay over there by the border so they gave them guns and food, and everything, to take for the Lao army camps. Each rebel camp took care of about 100 people – the rebel soldiers and some refugee people all stayed there together.

Most parts along the river there were communist soldiers and they watched it all day and all night. Everyday people got killed. Some people knew the parts where no one was watching – it was good to go across the border with someone who knew. Some people just watched the river and told the people who wanted to escape where the good part to cross was. They would tell the people who brought them the food when they were hiding in the jungle and they would tell other people. They knew where the army was today, where they would be tomorrow - they knew what parts the army was watching. Sometimes they lied, or they didn't know, and then you wouldn't make it. Some people died, you know? Oh, people died in the Mekong River every day, every night. Oh yep, I saw that – men, woman, kids, they killed all. It didn't matter. They died because they didn't know. People talked about it every day at the Lao army camps. The people that live by the Mekong River would tell everybody, "Oh, today 10 people floated past, today 20 people floated past." The bodies would just go down the river. Nobody could take care of the bodies, because everybody was scared, you know? How can you just go get some? You couldn't just go get some bodies out. I saw some go down the river when I crossed back and forth, but I couldn't do nothing. I just thought, "Someday I'm gonna die the same as them." I thought about that, and that's why I didn't want to stay with the rebel army at the camps no more. I just wanted to go stay at the refugee camp – the safe camp in Ubon.

I think it's still a little bit too dangerous to cross over the river to Laos – even driving, it's not good. In 2004 I heard that a bunch of people who were coming back from America got killed in Laos. They were riding on a bus to Laos from Thailand, but the communists shot them all. Everyone on the whole bus was killed. They were coming across the border in the south part of the country – it's not safe to cross down there – coming in through Vientiane is much better, so that's how I always go. It takes a lot, lot longer to get down south to my house in Pakse that way, but it's really a lot safer.

The communists are still all over in Laos looking for people because they are scared that people will come back now and start fighting again. I heard that they have names on a list and look for Lao people hiding in Thailand – if they find you in Thailand, they kill you in Thailand. They don't take you back to Laos to a camp no more. That's why Thailand put up the refugee camps along the border. They want the Lao people to control the border – they don't want to get involved. They want the rebel soldiers to watch the border and keep the Commies out…still.

So many people lost family during the war and never knew what happened to them. That's what happened to us with my oldest son. He left home one day in 1979 and said he was going to escape to Thailand and try to find his daddy. No one ever heard from him again. I still ask everyone I meet that was in the refugee camps if they ever saw him or know what happened to him. The answer is always, "Nope." I think he was probably killed. Oh, so many people were killed – too many. I feel sorry about that. The war, it was a very bad time for Lao people…very terrible. I can't talk about him, my son, anymore.

I am too sad about it.

5

Ubon's Wait Station

After I decided not to go back and help the rebels do fighting anymore, I stayed with the refugees at the Ubon camp in Thailand. The whole time I was there, I was thinking, "I want to go far away!" Many of the people there thought going to China was a really good idea because it was still in Asia, you know? I wanted to get away from all the fighting in Asia, they thought it was better to go there than to go far away to somewhere like France or America. But, you know, in 1992, sixty *thousand* people were sent back home by the Chinese government! They were all the people from the refugee camps that escaped from the war – all those people that asked them, "Can I go to China?" Yep, the Chinese, those guys sent them all back to the Commies in Laos. I knew it was a bad idea to ask to go to China!

Ubon's Wait Station

Whenever they interviewed me in the camp in Ubon I just kept saying, "I want to go to America." I didn't know anything about America, but I had worked with the American army soldiers and they were good guys, so I thought America must be a good place with good people in it. Yep, in 1979 I signed the paper in the refugee camp saying I wanted to go to America. That was it. I only wanted to go to America.

They taught English to everybody that wanted to come to America. If you wanted to go, you had to go to the school in the camp to learn English first. They asked you if you wanted to go to United States, then they asked you, "*Why* do you wanna come to the United States?" Some of the people had answers, but, "Wrong answer!" People with the wrong answers couldn't come.

Me, I told them the good answer. I told them I was a policeman. I told them I worked with the Americans. I said, "I don't want to stay in Thailand. I want to be American...like John Tiger!" I asked them, "Do you know that name?" Hahaha! "Oh, yeah, I know that name," they said. Our people called the big American soldier John Tiger. He worked at the embassy over there – he spoke Lao, Kampuchea, Vietnam – that guy, he could speak everything!

There was another American army guy I knew too. He worked in the army school for the Lao people – the people like me who learned to fight with the Americans. He controlled everything in the army school over there. They taught us Lao how to fight, you know? I forgot his name. Oh, I forgot that guy's name now. When I told them I knew John Tiger, they asked, "What? How do you know *him*??" And I just said, "Oh, I used to work with him." Hahaha! After I told them that they sent my name and my forms to Bangkok. A couple days later they told me, "Yep, you passed." Oh, I was a lucky guy! Hahahahaha! But you know, I was worried about my family in the camp going with me, too. I had a new wife with me I met in the camp…and a baby daughter born in there too.

You had to fill out lots of forms, and you had to talk with somebody that worked with the American embassy. Lots of our people, the Lao people, worked for the American embassy in the camp – in the Ubon camp. A lot of them worked for the doctors too. They helped the doctors, you know? A lot of American doctors were there. Most of the people that were there trying to help us in the camp were from America. They helped us with everything. They gave us everything, like food, and medicine. They really helped us a lot over there.

After I got the papers back from Bangkok that said, "Ok, you can go to America," we had to go to Bangkok and pass the test by doctors. I was worried about my new wife and daughter taking the doctor's tests because if you had something wrong in your body, you didn't pass the test. Something could be wrong and maybe you didn't know about it, you know?

After we got to Bangkok I stayed three nights there waiting to see the doctors. Then, after three days they called my name. We had to go to the doctor and get our bodies checked – they checked everything, you know? We had to take off *everything*, and... *hahaha, Oh my god!* I never did that kind of doctor test before! They checked us all together – boys and girls together. Oh my goodness! The men and women all had to take off *all* their clothes – the doctors had to check out your whole body. They checked everything! They took our blood out to do a test too. The doctors there they all spoke Lao to us because we didn't know too much English yet.

The Americans had the doctors in Bangkok send the whole group - about 200 people - to go to Hong Kong in an airplane together. There were refugees there from Vietnam, Kampuchea, and Laos. The people waiting together in Hong Kong came from all those different countries. I heard some people say all the monks, and some of the kids, died in the communist state. The monks tried to take care of the kids, but they all got killed. Under the communist state the kids and monks died. Some people said the kids died on the airplanes too, when America tried to get them out, but no one really knows why that happened, so people told me to be careful when I take the baby on the airplane.

The people who helped us with the papers in Bangkok explained to me what we had to do, so you know, *I knew* what we were doing, some people they didn't know what's going on. I knew we were going on the plane to America. I believed them. I trusted them that we were going to America. I wasn't scared or nothing. I knew they would never take me back to Laos, you know? I believed them because we fought together before. I didn't want to stay in Thailand because I wanted to go to the United States and see American money. Hahaha!

We went to Hong Kong and spent one night over there. We had to sleep in a special hotel. They put us ten people to one small room – just an empty room with a bathroom. We all had to sleep on the floor. In the morning they gave us each one big ball thing to eat. I

51

don't know what it's called…those things the Chinese make…a bun! Yeah, we each got one of those Chinese buns, but I didn't know how to eat it, so I watched another guy.

At eight o'clock in the morning a guy came to get me and put my family on an airplane to Alaska. I paid for that. I owed them $650 for me, my wife, and the baby, but the American embassy already paid ahead and reserved that plane for us. When I got a job here in the U.S. and made some money I paid them back. I paid the $650 back to them. I couldn't pay it all back at one time, though. They only made me pay $50 a month. I paid the government back because they needed the money to bring other people over here. Some people never paid back *nothing!* Ohhhh, really bad guys – those were the bad people!

There was more people on the plane, but only some of the refugees from the hotel in Hong Kong – not the public people. We couldn't see anything from the airplane, but it was early in the morning, and it was December. December 1980. We stopped in Alaska for about four or five hours, but I didn't get out of the plane. We had to stay stopped for awhile there but then the same plane took us to California. Then we had to stay three nights over there in California. They took us from the plane and put us all in the big hotel place for refugees again over there.

The whole hotel was just for the refugees. We couldn't go nowhere. Everyone had to stay in the hotel. We couldn't go outside or nothing – just stay in there and wait. They didn't have guards or anything to keep us in the hotel, but everybody was too scared to go out, so we just stayed in there. We were told, "Don't call *anybody!* Even if you have a cousin around here, or anybody, you can't call them. You just stay here!" They thought maybe if someone had the cousin or somebody near there they would come pick them up, and they didn't want us to just disappear, so we couldn't talk to nobody. I just said, "Ok, I don't know anybody. I'm not going nowhere."

I still had on my clothes from the refugee camp. In California, at the hotel, they gave me clothes and a jacket, gloves, and hat. It was donated stuff, or something like that, it wasn't brand new. Why would they give us brand new? Hahaha, no way! But it was ok - we came here with nothing, you know? We all had to wait there and everyone filled out the forms they needed and wait to go to the next place. Nobody knew where we going, but we knew we were in America and going somewhere else in America. After we filled out all the forms and gave them all our papers that they needed, we got to fly on the regular plane to the towns we were gonna live in.

They came to get me to put us on an airplane again, and I thought, "Oh my god, where are we going now?" They knew because they had our papers from our sponsors. We had the papers too, but couldn't read them, so how could we know? All the papers and forms we had to carry with us were all in English. Some people had papers from Thailand too, but all in English if we were going to America. They knew where we were going, but they didn't tell us, they just put us on the planes. The government paid for all that too – all the flights were included in the $650 I owed them.

From California, me, my wife, and daughter, we all flew to Chicago. Other refugees with us in California were sent to take that plane to Chicago with us too. When we got to the airport in Chicago we had to wait and then get on a plane that was smaller to go to our new town. We were the only refugee family to take the little plane to here.

6

Piles of Salt

W hen I got here I thought, "Yeaaa, I'm in The Freedom now!" That day was December 10th, 1980. That's my second birthday. That's the day I finished my long, long time travel to my freedom. After all the days I was waiting in the camps, and all the hotels, we were really getting to our new hometown, and starting a new life – in America!

I was so happy to get off that plane and see what kind of place we would be living in. Me and my wife were looking out the window on the plane when we were landing and thought the land looked really strange. She was holding the baby and she looked at me with the big eyes. We were both a little bit scared and we didn't know why the land looked so strange – we just couldn't figure it out! I told her it would be ok. When we got out of the airport and could walk outside we kept looking all around at the land. The ground was so white. Big piles of white stuff was piled up everywhere. It was clean on the walking path, but everywhere else was piles of white stuff. I never saw the ground like that before!

We were both really quiet and we were just looking, looking, then my wife, she asked me what all the white stuff was on the ground. She was really young and scared and didn't know nothing. I was supposed to know everything – I went to school, but we were in Laos, you know? We didn't have pictures of the ground like this in our school books. I said, "It must be salt. They must have so much salt around here that they have to pile it up on the ground!" I thought this must be a very rich place to have so many piles of salt. I thought, "Oh, they got a lot of salt here!" Yep, we must be in the really rich place to have so much salt that they have to pile it all up!

I thought about the camp, and about how we thought we were so lucky to get just a small, small, pinch of salt for our rice – it was the only flavor we got, and now this new country has so much salt it's piled up everywhere! I didn't know what the snow was then, or how it even looked like. We looked at the ground and it was all white. You know...*we* didn't know. I didn't know anything about the world. I only knew the jungle.

People here didn't know nothing about Laos back then, either. I will never forget about it – they would yell to me, "Hey Chinese, Chinese! Chong Chang, Chong Chang!" Hahaha! I thought what the heck? I didn't know what they were saying. I didn't know English too good, but I remember those words...Chong Chang, Chong Chang. I heard them all the time and tried to find them in my dictionary. I didn't know why they kept saying those same words all the time, and I couldn't find them in my book.

A church man sponsored me and my wife and our new baby. He was the same age as me, but I called him Dad, and I still do that. Dad was one English word I had learned before and it sounded a lot better to call him Dad than Mister, or Sponsor. He is my same age, but still, I call him Dad. He's my second father. Our sponsor met us at that little airport and took us to a two-story for us to live in. It was a scary neighborhood – not a good one, you know? My family lived in the first story and somebody lived in the second story. They were really noisy at the night time. Ohhhh I didn't know what was happening up there! I was still scared at night, oh yeah, still scared, because at night time when they were making all that noise up there. I thought, "What the heck? Am I living in the cemetery or something? I never saw anybody. I couldn't see nothing happening, I just heard a lot of noise all night.

In the morning my sponsor would come over and say, "Good morning!" I didn't know what he was saying. When he would talk to me in English I would just smile. Hahaha! When I got to the United States my sponsor got me a little book – a dictionary. My wife couldn't use it though. She can't read. I learned how to speak English from the book, and I went to school. I walked to an old school here that was close to my apartment where they taught new people English. My wife stayed home and took care of my kid. Some nights my sponsor came and took me and my wife and daughter to the school – we would go there together. My wife, she had to learn to speak English too. My Dad, he would check on me all the time and take us to the store once a week, and once a week he would take us to go do our laundry, too. He helped us a lot.

After a couple months I met another family from Laos through my sponsor, but at the English school I was the only one from Laos. There were a lot of people from all over, but not Laos…just me. The other guy I met from my sponsor, he was a policeman in Laos too, but he was from up north. He got here about a month before me. I asked how the people were here, and he said, "Some good, some bad." He didn't know nothing either. He lived in some apartments near me where other refugee families lived. One was from Kampuchea, and three from Laos. That guy, he escaped the way as me, but he escaped in the north. He was put in the jail the same as me, but it was a jail camp in the north. I don't know the story about the other refugee people at his apartment house.

I would walk around my neighborhood and sometimes people would say, "Hi," so I said, "Hi," but that's all, and just kept walking. That's all I could say. I didn't want to talk with them, you know, because I *couldn't* talk. I was scared when people said Hi. Some people just said, "Hi," but all the kids said, "Chinese! Chinese! Chong Chang, Chong Chang!" I thought, "Oh my god, what the heck are they doing? What did they say?" We didn't know nothing, you know. I was scared of those kids yelling at me, but my wife said, "Don't worry." Even when I drove my car around here, when I drove past them they yelled at me. Right now everyone all knows how to live together, and eh, no one says nothing bad to me no more. It's good here now...yep, it's really the good place for me now.

I feel lots better now. Now I know it was just the kids. They were just having fun, you know, so it's ok, and nobody says anything like that anymore. Before, when I would drive the car, or go to the store, or anything at all, kids would yell, "Hey Chong Chang!" They didn't know anything here before. Now I think they study more and learn from the schools. I tell them, "I am from Laos," and they say, "Where, where?" and I tell them it's by Thailand, Kampuchea, Burma...Vietnam, and then they *kinda* know where, and say, "Oh ok, ok." Some people from here went to the Vietnam War, so they heard about it. They know. Those people know, but still, most people don't know nothing about Laos. They have books in the library about it, and I think people should know now.

I lived in the first apartment house only about four or five months – then I moved to the government apartments in the bad part of town. I lived there for a year. Oh, I was really scared! It was really bad there – lots of shooting going on around there! One of my neighbor's sons got killed in there after I left. He was only about fourteen or fifteen, and got killed. He died in there. I moved to another apartment place and stayed there for awhile, then I bought my house – the one I still live in now. I bought it in 1989. I was doing good! I have some pet rabbits at my house and a garden where I grow the cucumbers, the peppers, long beans, everything! Yep, I'm not working anymore, but I'm doing real good.

My first job was working at a flower garden place – a greenhouse. I worked there for two years. My sponsor knew the owner and helped me get the job. Then, in 1983, it was on January 19th, I got the job at Vanchoe Animal Research Laboratory. I got the job over there because the owner there was another friend of my dad – my sponsor. The boss was nice to me. He knew who I was and where I came from, but the other people I worked with didn't know anything. They really didn't know nothing about me. When they asked where I was from and I said, "Laos," they didn't even know where that place was. They really knew nothing. It was only the owner of the company who knew something about Asia and where I come from.

I retired about ten times, but every year I could only stay retired for maybe four or five months and they would call me to come back to work more. They needed me there. They would call me to come back and I had to go because I needed the job still. I didn't have much other money. They always had a lot of jobs for me to do. I would go back for about six months – in the summer time I worked, and did everything they needed, then I got to be retired again and stay home for the winter. I worked there 28 years.

When I started the job there I didn't know nothing. I just worked. I worked in maintenance, but I didn't know what they did there, I just did what they told me. They would say, "Do this, do that," and I would just smile and say, "Ok." I did painting, cleaning, building doghouses with the wire…they used the cages I made for doghouses.

After they did the research on the dogs they sold them to Singapore. I don't know why Singapore wanted them. Maybe they ate them, I really don't know. Hong Kong and China also bought some dogs. After the company closed they sold all the animals and the equipment too. Besides Singapore and China they sold stuff to Vietnam and Japan too. They were shipping the animals everywhere. The animals shipped out every week. That's when I had to make a lot of cages. They only shipped one dog per cage, so I was very busy for months building the new shipping crates.

I built about 200 crates a week when they were shutting down the company and getting rid of all the old animals. They had about 800 dogs all together that they shipped out. They only sold the dogs they had done the research on that were still alive. They didn't ship the cats, but they did sell and ship all the rabbits too. I spent two years building rabbit cages for shipping. The rabbits were shipped in cages that could hold two. I think we sent about 200 rabbits to Asia. The rabbit cages I built out of cardboard with wire windows. The cats (about 100) they got rid of there at my work – they killed them and threw them away somewhere. Sometimes I saw dead ones, but not too many, so I really don't know what they did with them - they were all killed.

It looked like some kind of hospital in there. About once a month the doctor would come, and sometimes he would kill the animals. After he killed them the doctor would look inside them at their hearts and livers. I don't know how many people came with the doctor – maybe ten or fifteen. After they killed them and did the surgeries I had to take care of the bodies. I had to burn them. We had a big oven there they called "The Incinerator" I had to put all them in. They would bring me big bags of the dead animals to burn. About two or three hundred pounds would fit in The Incinerator at one time, and I burned them at 2,000 degrees.

Sometimes on the weekends when I wasn't at work they would put the dead rabbits outside. When I got there on Monday there was blood all over and they stunk *so* bad. Most of the time they killed them in the morning and I went to pick them up at noon. But, sometimes they would kill them over night. I don't know how they killed them when I was gone, but I know it made lots of blood. I had to wear a suit to cover my whole body to protect me from the germs. It was a big zip up suit...like a doctor's. I had to wear gloves, and goggles, and a hat. Sometimes they made me wear the gas mask too – like the soldiers in old wars.

All the rabbits that couldn't pass the doctor's tests were brought in a big bag to me and I had to kill them. I had to put them in The Incinerator. I didn't know I was killing them, but one day I turned up The Incinerator and put the bag in there and heard them yelling, "Help, help!" I ran out yelling for someone to come see it. I couldn't believe they were saying, "Help, help!" I couldn't believe it, and I was so scared! Someone came and told me the rabbits weren't dead yet, but I still had to burn them up. They brought them to me in the big black bags. I thought they were already dead, but no. I can still hear it, "Help, help, help," and all I could say was, "Oh, I'm so sorry." I didn't know what else I could do. I had to do it. Most of the time they just brought me the dead ones, but I guess sometimes they brought the ones that were still alive, too. They never brought me any of the dogs for burning, so I don't know how they got rid of them when they died. I only saw them kill the rabbits. They put them in a big glass tank and pumped some kind of gas in there to kill them. I guess sometimes the gas didn't kill them, and they would wake up screaming. I only saw that two times, but oh, I got so sick when I heard them calling for help.

I didn't know how to help, you know? I couldn't do nothing. They brought me the big bag with the rabbits in it and I had to put the whole thing in The Incinerator. I couldn't open the bags…never.

In the war I didn't want to kill nobody, but if I didn't kill them, they would kill me! I killed lots of people, but still I feel so bad about the rabbits. They cried for me to help them but I couldn't do nothing. I had to do it. I feel sorry about doing that. Yep, I'm still really sorry about it, but I couldn't save them, you know? I didn't like working there too much, but stayed because I needed the money. Money, money, everywhere you go, you know? Everything's so expensive to live here.

7

An American Returns

P eople all the time now ask me, "How is America?" I tell them I like it here. It's a lot better here, you know? It's a lot better than in Laos – better than I go to jail and eat one bowl of rice a day! I never thought about moving away from Laos before the war, but after the war started and then they put in the jail I thought about it…I thought about it *all* the time. I worked with Laos being a policeman, and in the war, and they paid me money you know, so it was ok. But oh, when they put me in jail, all I could think was, "How can I stay here? They are never gonna let me live." We were the same kind of people, like you and me now, you know? We should have worked together, but nope, they put me in the jail. They used to *pay* me! Why did they put me in the jail? Why didn't they keep me working?

An American Returns

In 1992, the Lao ambassador, he announced that anybody who wanted to go home could go. I wanted to go see my family, but I never thought about moving back there…never. I had enough money saved up to go back to Laos at that time, in 1992, so I just went for the visit, you know? I didn't want to live there again – no way! Many refugees returned then, and some stayed.

I only went to visit and stayed only one month. I went home to visit my mom, my dad, my cousins, and my old wife and our kids. That was the first year the government said people could come back to Laos. But oh, I was so scared! We didn't really know if it was gonna ok to go home or if we would all be killed. I was surprised at the airport because they were really friendly and thanked me when I arrived in Vientiane. The guard who checked my American passport and visa said, "Thank you for coming back to visit us." I wasn't so scared then. I just smiled to him and said, "Thank you!" Oh, I was so happy.

The big cities were kind of safe then because the government wanted people to come back home to make money, or bring money back from the other countries to give it to the families. I did take some money back to help my dad and everyone. I always send them money still. Not my dad because he is dead, but I send money to my kids and both my new wife's and old wife's mothers. I still want to help take good care of them.

In the small towns, people weren't so happy to see us refugees come back in 1992. There were still people hiding in Thailand back then and coming back across the river to fight for freedom. There were still small rebel groups trying to fight the communists, even in '92! It was easier for them to fight in the small towns. In the big cities they would have been killed right away. That made the small towns still a little bit dangerous. The people living in the small towns were still scared, too, and they would say, "Hey, you worked for the Americans!" I know they were scared to have us there. They were still scared of the government. The small town policemen watched us because they thought that maybe we were coming back there to join the rebels and fight again. That's why it wasn't safe to go to the small towns. It was better to stay in the big cities. It was safer there, but still *so* scary then!

I went to my small hometown the first time I returned to visit with my dad, but he said, "No, you can't stay here, you have to get back to the city," so I only stayed there one night and went back to town. We talked a little bit that night, my dad and me. He told me that he was glad I was an American now. He was really happy that I had the chance for the good life.

An American Returns

I had sent back a letter to my family from America a little while after I got here, and after the fighting quit a little bit in Laos. I was scared that maybe my letter would cause my family to get in trouble, but I sent it anyway. I had to tell them I was ok and that I was so sorry that I had to leave them. I sent it to my mother-in-law and she passed it around for all my family to read it. I got a letter from my father and it said to go back home. It came to my address, but I don't know how he got it there to me. My mother-in-law didn't live too far from my dad, so she must have told him my address and helped him. I wrote him a letter back. I told him, "Nope! I can't go back home! They will *kill* me! If I go back home they will kill me. You want me to die, or you want me to stay alive?" I said if I went back home they would kill me…Yep, kill me! I should have been careful. Talking bad about the government, even in the letters was not good to do, so I know my father, he just had to talk like that. They *had* to tell anybody they knew to go back home, you know? They had to say the things like that.

My dad wrote me back a couple times and said in the letters that I shouldn't have left and should come back to Laos. That was about all he said because he couldn't say much. He was scared to send the letter too. If somebody from the government got the letters he might get in trouble if he said anything bad about the new Lao government. So when I got to his house that day in '92 to finally see him again I said I was sorry I hadn't come home like he told me. He said he didn't really want me to come back there, and he was happy and proud that I made it all the way to America.

It was the only time I got to see him – in 1992 – that's when they sent all the people from the refugee camp that went to China back to Laos. They wanted everybody all back home. When I saw him I talked about the letter and he said, "Oh, I just talked about it, you know I didn't mean it." He just told me to go back home in case somebody got his letter – he tried to write the letter real careful. He said, "I'm glad you didn't come back – they killed lots of people" And I said, no, I didn't want to come back either. You had to be careful even just talking in 1992. You had to be real careful.

He was happy I was American. I gave him some money, not much, just a little bit, but he was happy. He was already sick then, but I had sent money for him with a friend of mine that was going to Laos from America, and that made him happy, a little bit. He got a little bit of freedom from the money I sent to him, and he got to go to the doctor. Because I was sending him money, he finally got to go to the doctor…a *real* doctor in the big city.

An American Returns

My mom passed away in 1974. I think she had cancer or something like that. We never knew back then. My dad lived longer – until he was 86. He died in 1996. I think he had lung cancer, but really nobody knew what kind of the illness the people had back then. My parents still lived in a small town when they died. Everyone was poor and poor people couldn't go to the big cities to go to hospitals. We didn't have hospitals in the small villages, and my dad had no money to go to the city. They had some small clinics there in the small towns, but all they might give you is an aspirin or something. They didn't have anything there, so really there was no use. After I sent the money from the U.S. to my dad, he went to Pakse to get x-rays done there. They talked to him about lung cancer, but I don't know. He had been sick a long time and had a headache all the time.

I saw my dad in '92 the first time I went back. That was the last time I got to see him. He died after that and I didn't have a passport to go sooner because they were so expensive then. It was about $5,000 for the three of us to go back that first time. I had to save everything – all of my money. So, yep, 1992 was the last time I saw my dad. When I went back after that, and every time since then, I make a party, like a ceremony for them, my parents. I miss them so much. Oh, it's sad for me. I really miss them a lot, you know? But they are gone, so now I just try to take care of my sister. She has no husband so she don't have the family. She just stays in our mother and father's old house by herself. I get to see my old wife, and my youngest daughter, and my son, too when I go back. They don't live too far from each other, so I get to go to visit with them all now.

A friend of mine called me one time from Thailand to give me a message from my family – they didn't have phones over there in Laos, so people had to cross the border to make the phone calls. Before we didn't have any phones – no nothing in Pakse, or even in the big city like Vientiane – they didn't have no phones there either. Before 1992 no phones, no nothing, just the government had the phones, you know? Nobody had phones in Laos – just the government buildings had the phones in them. The people had no phone, no nothing. They had to go to the Thailand border and cross over there to make the call. But now? Oh, everybody has cell phones now – just like me here. They still don't have no house phones, but everybody has the cell phone. Even the poor people have the cell phones now. They can just pay a little bit and use it for maybe a week.... if you don't talk too much. I think the Thai companies own the cell phone companies Laos.

A lot of Thai people that have money want to open a business in Laos now because they don't tax you for seven years if you start a business there. The government is kind of open now. Its better – better than nothing, you know? Lao people are getting jobs – learning from Thai companies how to build the houses, and buildings, and everything! People still try to grow their own food and have their own animals – you know, they like to have their own farms, but new Lao people are a lot better than before. They are doing lots better! Lots of people from the other countries in Asia: Malaysia, Singapore, Hong Kong, Indonesia, they go to make business over there. They start the new companies. After the old communist leader passed away, the original one, we got a new government and they changed a little bit – things got better. He was still in charge until about 1992, when I went there. Then he died and a new president took over the communist government and it got lots better.

One time four or five of us that had studied together at the monastery met to drink beer together when I went back. One of them asked me, "How did you escape to Thailand? Why did you escape to Thailand?" I told them, "Oh, they put me in the jail, and I didn't want to stay there," I said. How could I stay? I never had freedom, you know? I was thinking that I was gonna die over there. They were all just laughing, you know. When I started going back home my family and friends didn't want to talk about the war – they just keep quiet about it. Before, when I first started going back over there, I didn't want to talk either, so I would just keep quiet too. I didn't want them to know, you know?

People still don't talk about the war. They talk about studying a lot right now. Everybody talks about studying to get a job. More people worry about business and money now. They don't want to talk or hear about the bad time no more. The government doesn't want to hear people talk about that either – they don't want people sticking together. They don't want the fighting to start the same as before.

Lao people's life right now is good. They are doing really good. Some people got a lot of money now and start a business like build their own hotel or something. I don't know where they get that much money from. A friend of mine (we studied together in 1960), right now he has a resort and a big house, and a car, and everything! I studied with him in the monastery. We went to school together about 45 or 46 years ago, something like that. He's doing really good now. I talked to him on the phone when we were all drinking together, and yep, he still knew me! I first saw him again in about 2008. He's known me for a real long time now.

When I go to visit now my friends just want to drink beer and have a good time. Other people, they want me to bring clothes, shoes, everything, but I only bring for my family – to help them get better – I don't want to give to everybody. Right now when I go home everybody says, "Oh, I need the clothes, I need the jacket, I need something." Everybody wants something. Some people want the cell phone, "Oh, I need the phone. Can you buy one for me?" Nope, I don't think so. How can I buy that? It's still expensive: $50. They think I am rich because I am American. Yep, that's what they think. They know I am American and everybody wants to come to America right now. They want to make some money, you know, then go back home. Some people that came here made like thirty or forty thousand and then took the money back home to make a new business. Yep, if you got thirty, maybe forty thousand dollars you can go there and have a nice car – Toyota, Honda, some nice car like that – you can get *everything* if you got that much money!

When I go back home I feel bad that I don't have the car over there. I feel bad because I don't have anything much like I do here. I don't even have what they have *there* now! They have everything now, you know. Over there I feel poor. Hahaha! Here I feel ok. I feel I'm in the middle here – it's ok, everybody can be the same. I feel poor there, but everybody thinks I am rich. All the time I hear the young ladies say, "Bring me, bring me! Please take me over there. I want to go with you!" I tell them, "No, I can't take you, I got a wife, I am married, and I don't even have a job now." They all want to come here. I think everybody in Laos still wants to come to America…they think everything is easy here, but no, that's not true.

I used to have to get a new passport every two years. They always made me get the new, new, new…old passports you can't keep, so I don't know all the times I went back there now. But now its lots better – I get the passport that I can use for 10 years because I am a citizen now, not like before. Now I'm an American, same as you. I became a citizen in 2001 or 2002…I forget the year. If you're not the citizen you still have to get a new one every two years – like my wife, she's just the resident still. She's the permanent resident though.

The first time I took my wife back to Laos was 1998. We were excited and scared to see everybody back home – we were both, both scared, and happy. We took one of my daughters with us too. We took our oldest one. She was the only one born in Thailand. She was born in the camp in Thailand in 1980 and came here with us when she was a little baby. My youngest one, our youngest daughter, was born here in 1983. She didn't want to go so she stayed here. She didn't want to go because her mom told her there were no bathrooms over there…the bathroom is in the jungle – in the field, the rice field. She was only nine years old, but she said, "Nope, I'm not doing that!" So my daughter said she wasn't going. Even here she won't go camping or nothing if there is no bathroom, so she stayed here with my sponsor.

If you go to the bathroom over there, you have to go outside, so you have the dogs and pigs running all over…hahahahha! We go to the bathroom in the rice field – that's how everybody goes to the bathroom there. But now? Oh they have a lot of bathrooms inside the house now in the cities. Oh, that's really good! But outside the big towns, they still go to the bathroom the same way: outside in the field. It's easy, but the smell is bad. When it's raining some people take the umbrella, but some people can't because they don't have one. A lot of people are still really poor. Here, everybody has the umbrella.

In 2004 my whole family went to Laos all together - my oldest daughter had the wedding over there. She got married here, but wanted to have the Lao style wedding too. We stayed for three weeks. I talked with my son and we made a plan that he would take care of getting a house built there for me. I sent him money from America and he took care of everything for me.

I have a big house there now – it's really big and nice too, you know – all wooden floors and everything. In my new house I built over there I have a bathroom. I have two bathrooms! The lower one is a really good one. It has the tile floor and the bath tub in it too, oh really nice! Upstairs I didn't put in the tub - just only the shower, but it's all tile too. Some people still just have the faucet that comes out the wall and fills the big vase with water and use the bowl to scoop out the water and wash that way. My son still does it that way even with the shower in my house: he just uses the shower to fill bucket and then pour the water on him with the bowl. In the countryside they still do it that way too, but some inside, some still outside. Most people just have the big vase outside to fill with the water, and they take the shower outside, too.

When I was young some people have the outside shower like that, but some of us just have the Mekong River – just go outside and jump in! My house was not too far from the river – it was only about fifty feet from my house to the Mekong River, so we just walk down there and jump in. Some people were a little bit further from the river, but everyone tried to build the houses close to it. If people live far from the river they have to dig the big well to get to the water, and they collect the rain. All the small towns were the same – they just have one big well and everybody has to use to get the water for everything – washing, cooking, everything – all the people in the village share that. All the small towns away from the river are still like that, but now they have the motor to pump the water up in to a tank, you know? At my big house there we have our own well with a big motor for pumping the water…just for our house.

In 2009 I spent six months over there building my wife's mom a house there too. I went there to see my new house and build her a new one. My wife's mom's house doesn't have a well though. She uses the public well. All the water that comes out of the ground, we still have to boil it there – it's not clean enough for drinking – the ground and the water is still all poison in it from the war. In the north there's still a lot, a lot, of bombs in the ground there. I don't know what they do about it. I don't know what they do when they need to get the water out. I don't know how they can live. I didn't go up there for a long time. It's far away, from my house there, you know? I think it must be too hard for the people to live up there.

When I think about myself now, I think, "I am ok." That's the first thing I think of. I am better than before, you know? I have retirement money back again, the same like before – I worked for the government there and was gonna have a retirement someday, but right now I have my retirement from here and I think, "Oh, this is lots better!" Hahaha! It's a lot better than the money I would have got over there, you know? I don't have a lot, about $1,500 a month, but it's ok. The government retirement over there is only about two or three hundred dollars a month. My policeman job had a retirement too – but they don't have as much as the Americans that get the retirement money.

My cousin who worked for the policemen, he died in the prison camp, but his wife lives here in the U.S. now. Her and four of their sons all got to come here. She got here in about 1990. She came over right from Laos. She said the American government asked if any people wanted to get out. They helped. They took some people out and brought them to the U.S. on airplanes. My daughter Chanh came here that way too. Not like me, I had to walk! Hahaha! Chanh has been here for ten or fifteen years now. The government doesn't help anybody get out no more though. If you want to come to America now, you have to have a family member who is a citizen…like me! One of my cousin's sons that escaped to Thailand went to France. I never saw him again.. I never saw a lot people again. My family had a real hard time in the war. It's not right to do, but still, I wanted to tell my story, you know?

Epilogue...

Developing a print voice for Casey's reminiscences and maintaining consistency of that voice throughout the memoir was undoubtedly the primary (and naively unforeseen) challenge of the preceding project. Casey's memories and monologues were transformed by the lengthy tasks of dictation, transcription, analysis, and editing. Convergence of his input and my output created a distinct third voice which became an entity of its own - sentenced to exist wholly between prologue and epilogue. I feel I have succeeded in presenting his story in the manner which he intended it to be heard.

Many of the difficult editorial decisions I had to make were resultant of the story being told by a narrator who was asked to recount experiences that took place many decades ago. Events were disclosed in random sequence, and often repeated, with varying details. When such discrepancies arose, he was asked to clarify the story; the response then added yet another account of the same event. Due to the subjectivity of memory, as relative to storytelling, I found it best to utilize creative editorial license in recreating the event(s) from a combination of the given narratives, rather than pressing the narrator for a definitive "final account" of any events. Conclusively, the long-standing, close relationship between Casey and I afforded me the ability to comfortably make all necessary editorial decisions.

Our personal relationship was also critical in producing the life history account itself. Creation of the memoir relied on a multitude of processes, and aspects of his life and relationships, including the one between narrator and ethnographer; the importance of which should not be underestimated[21]. Thus, being subjective to a variety of variables, the comfort level of participants is paramount. From a processualist viewpoint, the very experience of telling one's life history to another is an important psychological process within which the story is both created from, and an outcome of, life events coupled with dialogue.[22] It is also noteworthy that Casey had never shared any of the details regarding his life history with another person, and longed to do so. Accordingly, I trust the events were narrated sincerely, regardless of variation.

Interestingly, since concluding our interview phase of the process, Casey has not initiated any dialogue regarding his past; which was the primary topic of our

---

[21] James Peacock and Dorothy Holland. "The Narrated Self: Life Stories in Process." *Ethos,* (1993): 376.
[22] *Ibid.,* 371.

personal conversations over the past decade. The focal point of our conversations, post-interview period, became the present and future. He now emphasizes his future plans, and repeatedly mentions a desire to immigrate back to Laos. This is conceivably the most telling sign that he has reconciled with the ills he endured during the war, himself, and perhaps most notably, with the motherland he had risked his life to depart. Aside from repeatedly expressing his wish to repatriate to Laos, he has diligently attempted to persuade me to spend time in Laos to experience first-hand the land I have gotten to know through years of research and anecdotes.

Given the nature of the events he was asked to recount, maintaining close observation of his behavior during and after the interviews for signs of distress was ethically an obligatory practice on my part. After reflecting on the unexpected change of dynamics in our relationship regarding conversational topics, I have deduced that the disclosure of long-kept secrets was a transformative process in which he became unencumbered by past experiences, resulting in a reconciliatory solace. Also, as a result of our months spent together in interviews, a more permanent bond has developed between us. Our relationship has become one of life-long confidants; whereas the previous dynamic of our friendship was less intimate.

Gaining access to subjects one wishes to interview is often the most difficult and deciding factor to embarking on an oral history-based ethnographic project. A degree of insider status, as perceived and granted by the individual(s) being interviewed, is helpful in achieving a level of trust and honesty essential to such a project. However, straddling the threshold of insider/outsider proved to be most efficacious in my particular instance.

The project's narrator had been raised in a culture in which speaking of the past, tragedy, or the dead, was a cultural taboo; therefore he would not have been willing to share details of his story with another member of his home-culture group due to the cultural constraints regarding language and information-sharing. Due to the aforementioned reasons, Casey agreed to tell his stories on the condition that his participation in the project remain unbeknownst to his family and friends until it was published.

While my outsider status was necessary for the story to be shared, decades of involvement in the local Southeast Asian immigrant community afforded me a type of insider status which also facilitated access. Also of necessity was the mutual trust and respect Casey and

I shared, and my knowledge of the cultural proprieties and practices, history, and language; for without those proficiencies the preceding oral history-based biography would not have reached fruition.

Concluding our final interview, I thanked Casey for the many months of hard work and wonderful storytelling. I promised to keep him up to date on the project and supply him with a copy of the finished product to which he simply replied, "No thank you, I am all done now," and smiled.

Questions for Discussion:

1) What is the significance of the book's title?

2) Discuss the pros and cons of the author's choice to recreate the story in 1st person format, as it was initially told. How would the impact of the story have changed had it been written in 3rd person?

3) What does it say about the narrator that he chose an American pseudonym for himself, yet chose Laotian names for all others in his story?

4) What could you attribute the lack of elaborate descriptions Casey used in his storytelling to?

5) How has your view of immigration and immigrants in the United States been affected by Casey's story?

REFERENCES & FURTHER READINGS

Barkan, Elliott R. "America in the Hand, Homeland
   in the Heart: Transnational and Translocal Immigrant
   Experiences in the American West." *The Western
   Historical Quarterly*, vol. 35, no. 3 (2004): 331-354.

Becker, Gay, Beyene, Yewoubdar, and Ken, Pauline.
   "Memory, Trauma, and Embodied Distress: The
   Management of Disruption in the Stories of Cambodians
   in Exile." *Ethos*, vol. 28, no. 3 (2000): 320-345.

Benard, Cheryl. "Politics and the Refugee Experience."
   Political Science Quarterly, vol. 101, no. 4 (1986):
   617-636.

Berlinski, C. "The Dark Figure of Corruption." *Policy
   Review*, no. 155 (2009): 71-81.

Bornat, Joanna. "Reminiscence and Oral History: Parallel
   Universes or Shared Endeavour?" *Ageing and Society,*
   (2001): 215-241.

Brown, Mac Alister and Zasloff, Joseph. "Laos 1978: The
   Ebb and Flow of Adversity." *Asian Survey*, Vol. 19, No.
   2, A Survey of Asia in 1978: Part II (1979): 95-103.

Charlton, T., Myers, L., and Sharpless R., eds. *Thinking
   about Oral History*. USA: AltaMiraPress, 2008.

Cohon, J. Donald Jr. "Psychological Adaptation and
   Dysfunction among Refugees." *International Migration
   Review*, vol. 15, no. 1/2 (1981): 255-275.

Conquergood, Dwight. "Health Theatre in a Hmong Refugee
   Camp: Performance, Communication, and Culture."*TDR,*

Bibliography

vol. 32, no. 3 (1988): 174-208.

Daniels, Roger. *Guarding the Golden Door: American Immigration Policy and Immigrants Since 1882.* New York: Hill & Wang, 2004.

Davy, Joseph. "Repatriation: How Safe is it?" *Hmong Studies Journal*, 2(2), (1998):1-10.

Dinh, Nathalie M. H. and Groleau, Danielle. "Traumatic Amputation: A Case of Laotian Indignation and Injustice." *Culture, Medicine and Psychiatry*, no. 32 (2008):440–457.

Edwards, Scott. "The Refugee in International Society." *Political Science Quarterly*, vol. 124 (2010): 757-758.

Evans, Grant. *The Politics of Ritual and Remembrance.* Honolulu: University of Hawai'i Press, 1998.

Evans, Grant (Ed.). *Laos Culture and Society.* Bangkok: O.S. Printing House, 1999.

Fass, Simon. "Through a Glass Darkly: Cause and Effect in Refugee Resettlement Policies. *Journal of Policy Analysis and Management*, vol. 5 (1985): 119-137.

Fass, Simon. "Innovations in the Struggle for Self-Reliance: The Hmong Experience in the United States." *International Migration Review*, vol. 20, no. 2, Special Issue: Refugees: Issues and Directions (1986): 351-380.

Gupta, Akhil, and Ferguson, James. "Beyond "Culture": Space, Identity, and the Politics of Difference." *Cultural Anthropology*, vol. 7, no. 1 (1992): 6-23.

Harrell-Bond, B. E and Voutira ,E. "Anthropology and the Study of Refugees." *Anthropology Today*, vol. 8, no. 4 (1992): 6-10.

Head, William P. "Playing hide-and-seek with the trail: Operation Commando Hunt 1968-1972." *Journal of Third World Studies*, 19 (1), (2002): 101-115.

Hein, Jeremy. "Refugees, Immigrants, and the State." *Annual Review of Sociology,* vol. 19 (1993): 43-59.

Howell, David R. "Refugee Resettlement and Public Policy: A Role for Anthropology. *Anthropological Quarterly*, vol. 55, no. 3 (1982): 119-125.

Huyck, Earl and Bouvier, Leon. "The Demography of Refugees." *Annals of the American Academy of Political and Social Science*, vol. 467 (1983): 39-61.

Ingleby, David (Ed.). *Forced Migration and Mental Health.* New York: Springer, 2005.

Kelly, Gail P. "Coping with America: Refugees from Vietnam, Cambodia, and Laos in the 1970s and 1980s." *Annals of the American Academy of Political and Social Science*, vol. 487 (1986): 138-149.

Khamvongsa, Channapha & Russell, Elaine. "Legacies of War: Cluster Bombs in Laos. *Critical Asian Studies,* vol. 41, no. 2 (2009): 281–306.

Kunz, E. F. "The Refugee in Flight: Kinetic Models and Forms of Displacement." *International Migration Review*, vol. 7, no. 2 (1973): 125-146.

LeCompte, M.D. "The Transformation of Ethnographic Practices: Past and Current Challenges." *Qualitative Research*, 2(3), (2002): 283-299.

Marcus, George E. "Ethnography in/of the World System:

Bibliography

The Emergence of Multi-Sited Ethnography." *Annual Review of Anthropology,* Vol. 24 (1995): 95-117.

Nasstrom, Kathryn L. "Pushing Boundaries in Oral History-Based Biographies." *The Oral History Review,* Vol. 32, Issue 2 (2005): 77-81.

Ong, Aihwa. *Buddha is Hiding*. Berkley: University of California Press, 2003.

Palmer, David. "Every Morning before You Open the Door You Have to Watch for that Brown Envelope: Complexities and Challenges of Undertaking Oral History with Ethiopian Forced Migrants in London, U.K." *The Oral History Review*, vol. 37 (2010): 35-53.

Peacock, James L. and Holland, Dorothy C. "The Narrated Self: Life stories in Process." *Ethos,* vol. 21, no. 4 (1993): 367-383.

Pholsena, V. *Post-war Laos*. Ithaca: Cornell University Press, 2006.

Rumbaut, Rubén G. "Paradoxes (and Orthodoxies) of Assimilation." *Sociological Perspectives*, vol. 40, no. 3 (1997): 483-511.

Rumbaut, Rubén G. "Ages, Life Stages, and Generational Cohorts: Decomposing the Immigrant. First and Second Generations in the United States." *International Migration Review*, vol. 38, no. 3 (2004): 1160-1205.

Savanda, Andrea. *Laos a Country Study*. Washington, D.C.: U.S. Government Printing Office, 1995.

Stein, Barry. "The Refugee Experience: Defining the Parameters of a Field of Study." *International*

Migration Review, vol. 15, no. 1/2 (1981): 320-330.

Suedfeld, Peter. "Reactions to Societal Trauma: Distress and/or Eustress." *Political Psychology*, vol. 18, no. 4 (1997): 849-861.

Tafarodi, R., Lo, C., Yamaguchi, S., Lee, W.S., and Katsura, H. "The Inner Self in Three Countries." *Journal of Cross-Cultural Psychology*, (2004): 35:97.

Thompson, Paul. *The Voice of the Past.* Oxford: Oxford University Press, 2000.

Tollefson, James W. "Functional Competencies in the U.S. Refugee Program: Theoretical and Practical Problems." *TESOL Quarterly*, vol. 20, no. 4 (1986): 649-664.

Van der Veer, Guus. *Counselling and Therapy with Refugees and Victims of Trauma.* West Sussex: John Wiley & Sons Ltd., 1998.

Viraphol, S. "Reflections on Thai-Lao Relations." *Asian Survey*, vol. 25, no. 12 (1985): 1260-1276.

Waters, Mary C. and Jiménez, Tomás. "Assessing Immigrant Assimilation: New Empirical and Theoretical Challenges. *Annual Review of Sociology*, vol. 31 (2005): 105-125.

Weinstein, Gail. "Literacy and Second Language Acquisition: Issues and Perspectives." *TESOL Quarterly*, vol. 18, no. 3 (1984): 471-484.

Wheeler, Norton. "Gaining Access and Sharing Authority: What I learned about Oral History from an Episode in U.S.-China Transnationalism." *The Oral History Review*, vol. 31, no. 2 (2004): 53-68.

ACKNOWLEDGMENTS

Thank you Lung for sharing your time, your unending kindness, and your story with me. You are a true friend and have my utmost respect.

Thank you Dr. Vincent Lyon-Callo, Dr. Kristina Wirtz, and the Anthropology department at WMU for the years of camaraderie, encouragement, and superior mentorship.

Thank you family and friends who read each draft of this manuscript and continually encouraged its publication.

Thank you Kory and Klay for being the prime instigators of my adventurous spirit and fortitude. I love you.

Thank you dad for consistently seeing the good in people, giving so selflessly to others, and for always saying you were proud of me. I wish you were here. I miss you.

Mom, I miss you too. Thanks for the independence.

ABOUT THE AUTHOR

Patrice Niltasuwan is a college professor with an M.A. in Cultural Anthropology from Western Michigan University. She has an intense interest in the human condition and American immigrant culture in particular. A passion for Asia and Far Eastern Thought has led her to travels throughout Thailand, China, and Inner Mongolia. *Piles of Salt,* her first publication, is a true labor of love intended to promote greater intercultural understanding and brotherhood.